T0383507

MOnsters

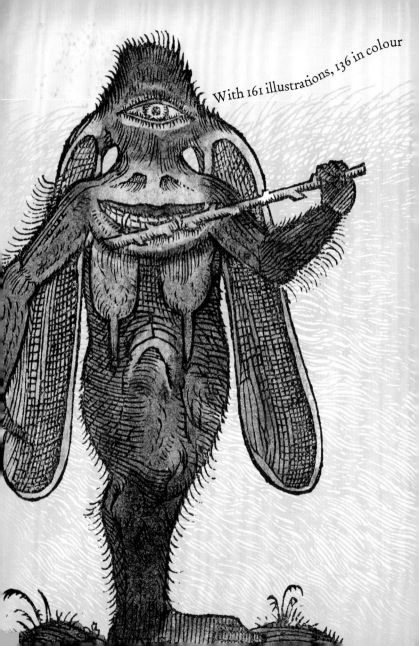

With 161 illustrations, 136 in colour

Christopher Dell

MOnsterS

A BeStiaRy of the BizaRre

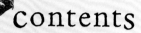

contents

iN the BegiNNiNG ...

> " Echidna conceived and brought forth fierce offspring; first she gave birth to Orthus, the hound of Geryones, and then ... a monster called Cerberus who eats raw flesh, the hound of Hades, fifty-headed, relentless and strong. And she gave birth to a third, the evil-minded Hydra of Lerna ... She was the mother of Chimaera, who breathed raging fire, a creature fearful, great, swift-footed and strong, who had three heads, one of a grim-eyed lion; in her hindpart, a dragon; and in her middle, a goat ... "

And so the monsters were born – according to the ancient Greeks, at least. This vivid passage comes from Hesiod's epic poem *Theogony,* composed in about 700 BC. The mother, Echidna, was herself a monster, half python and half nymph. Living underground, she was descended from gods, but the line had mutated. Her offspring are a mismatched jumble of parts, fit only for terrorizing people: the hellish Cerberus, the multiheaded Hydra, the deadly Sphinx.

Though heroes soon came to destroy these beasts and to restore normality, it was too late: the monsters had already seized our imaginations.

Today they have multiplied beyond Hesiod's wildest dreams, and we are plagued by minotaurs, dog-headed gods, werewolves, centaurs, harpies, sea monsters, tentacled aliens, mermaids, trolls, ogres, devils, demons and cyclopes – to name just a few. Every single culture on earth has its own monsters, and the more that we learn about them, the more fascinating they become. Their stories, their curious habits and diets, and the ways in which they can be warded off create a picture of imaginations running riot. What does the existence of monsters, even if only in our heads, say about humankind? How have they survived the millennia, and why are they universal? Why do we find the same one-eyed giants in Japan and in ancient Greece, or the same dragons in Europe and in China?

One reason is that monsters answer to a sense of the supernatural that lies deep within us. This has been true since the earliest times – certainly, the religions of Egypt and Mesopotamia revelled in monsters and demons, with even their gods appearing monstrous to modern eyes. The battle between order and chaos, between good and evil, was made visible through gods and monsters.

Even when monsters are described in words,
it is their appearance that matters most – the
number of heads or eyes, the spikiness of the tail,
the sharpness of the fangs. As this book shows, artists
have always loved depicting monsters. Indeed, the
earliest cave art includes animal–human hybrids
that must have had a considerable impact on those
who first saw them: could they
really exist out there, beyond
the cave?

Monsters are
creatures that go against
the laws of nature.
They have many sources: mythology, religious
texts and traditions, folklore, and even literature.
They tend to combine human and animal parts,
although many – griffins and dragons, for example –
are composites of different animals, and the human
aspect is frequently reduced to the possession of
a scheming mind. Others, such as werewolves,
constantly switch between forms. The human bearing
of these creatures deliberately raises disturbing
questions. Are they thinking? Can they talk?
What else might they be capable of?

In ancient Egypt and Mesopotamia, monsters
were a fact of life, and we can assume that the people
of those times believed implicitly in their physical

reality. The three great monotheistic
religions, Judaism, Christianity and Islam,
were more reluctant to discuss monsters.
The Old Testament generally excludes the type
of supernatural beings included here (although
it does mention the giant land and sea monsters
Behemoth and Leviathan). In the New Testament, the
Revelation of St John contains the famous description
of the Seven-Headed Beast, but Christianity's
monsters most often appear in later stories – St George
jousting with the dragon, for example,
or the ferocious Tarasque tamed
by St Martha.

In the pagan world of ancient
Greece and Rome, everything had a far more
fluid form. In his *Metamorphoses*, the poet
Ovid catalogues a seemingly endless tit-for-tat of
the gods, as they turn each other (and a fair proportion
of humanity) into other creatures.

Indeed, the world of Classical mythology offers the most fertile terrain for monsters. Where else could a woman infatuated with a bull give birth to a creature half man, half bull?

In fact, the story of Durga in Hindu legend tells of something very similar (although here it is a man who falls in love with a cow). The gods of Hinduism, like those of the ancient Egyptians, are very often depicted as alterations of the human form – some have extra limbs, another has an elephant's head, and others still have supernatural and shape-shifting powers. Its demons, too, are plentiful and potent. This pattern is repeated on the other side of the globe, in the Olmec culture of the Americas. Here, as in Egypt, priests would temporarily take on monstrous characteristics by dressing up.

Folk stories tell of trolls and giants, mermaids and mermen, fairies and leprechauns, werewolves and vampires. We find such traditions in Native American mythology, as well as in China, Japan, Africa and throughout Europe – every culture, in fact, has its own folk monsters. Some lurk in dark places but others watch over us; some unusual Japanese sprites even clean our bathrooms while we sleep.

Medieval Europe was still full of superstition and fear. Monsters could now be in the home (in the form of devils and demons) or in far-away lands (creatures with faces in their torsos, and with one leg and three eyes). Such beings appeared regularly in sculpted capitals and in the margins of manuscripts, causing St Bernard of Clairvaux to condemn what he termed 'monstrous deformities and deformed monstrosities'. More acceptable were bestiaries, which related moral tales involving animals such as unicorns.

This fascination with monsters continued into the Renaissance. Even after Columbus's travels, there remained places to explore and discoveries to be made. The new discipline of science initially attempted to categorize and to explain monsters – leading to the hundreds of badly stitched-together grotesques we find in 'cabinets of curiosity' – but by the 17th century scientists were beginning to have serious doubts. Cartographers discreetly started to remove the scaly sea monsters from the edges of their maps, embarrassed that they had ever been allowed in.

But in the 18th century Europe experienced a new interest in monsters, spurred on by Romanticism. The immediate masterpiece of this new movement was Mary Shelley's *Frankenstein* (1818) – perhaps the first real psychological insight into what it was to *be* a monster. As the century progressed, the genre of Gothic horror seized the public's imagination, catapulting figures such as Dracula into the general consciousness. Nor were children spared this barrage, as we can see from the stories of the Brothers Grimm, populated with grisly creatures.

In Japan, folklore began to take on a vivid (and often humorous) new form, as seen in 18th-century depictions of 'The Night Parade of A Hundred Demons', which brought together an impressive range of bizarre creatures. This creativity was matched in North America, where a fresh set of monster myths was emerging as the great migration towards the West Coast penetrated unknown mountains and timberlands. Referred to as the 'fearsome critters', these new creatures included the glawackus, the hodag, the squonk and the jackalope.

Technology soon bred its own monsters, with H. G. Wells's Dr Moreau playing god to create mutant hybrids of animals and humans. The early 20th century brought the first real explanations of why we need monsters. Jung, in particular, believed that monsters were essential to our development, relaying to us important messages about our psychological state and representing the 'otherness' within ourselves, the division between 'a bright day-world and a dark night-world peopled with fabulous monsters'.

From Picasso's minotaurs to Jorge Luis Borges's *Handbook of Fantastic Zoology*, people's interest in monsters seemed to continue unabated. The field of cryptozoology – the study of creatures that might

or might not exist – has grown dramatically, and today embraces everything from the Loch Ness Monster to the Yeti, from Bigfoot to the *chupacabra* – all of which have supposedly been sighted and photographed in recent years.

The growth of science fiction over the last century has led to a new breed of monsters, this time from outer space (though still suspiciously anthropomorphic). Perhaps this is a signal that we are beginning to exhaust the possibilities of monsters on our planet, forcing us to turn our eyes to the infinite blackness.

Resistance to monsters is clearly futile. While we may no longer worry about being eaten by trolls on the way home, there remains a fascination with, and fear of, these creatures that have shadowed us throughout history. After all, we should remember who created them: not the gods, nor Echidna, but man. Above all else, this book is a testament to humankind's incredible, fevered, indestructible imagination.

pages 1-14
KEY TO ILLUSTRATIONS

1. GODS and MONSTERS

Gods and monsters are essential companions – and, as the story of Echidna in the introduction shows, they are often even related. The one-eyed Cyclopes were the children of the gods Uranus and Gaia, as were the Giants, colossal creatures sometimes depicted with snakes in place of legs. These monsters, unsatisfied with their lot, attempted to storm Olympus and to overthrow the gods. Family relations did not improve with the birth of Saturn, who castrated and cast out his father, then in turn devoured his own children to prevent them from seizing power.

From the earliest times, it has been difficult to distinguish between gods and monsters: both are supernatural, existing beyond the realms of day-to-day experience, and both demand and inspire fear. Many deities, of course, appear monstrous in their own right. God-type creatures from the Trois Frères caves in south-west France show liminal beings that

combine human and animal elements to terrifying effect. Painted in around 14,000 BC, they must have played an important role in shamanistic ceremonies held deep underground. Groping in the darkness, initiates would have made out creatures that they had never seen. The ancient Egyptian gods, with their animal heads, are clearly also designed to intimidate the devout, to underline the gods' existence in another realm; in his *Aeneid*, Virgil writes disdainfully of the Egyptians' 'monstrous gods of every form, and barking Anubis'.

Intimidation is found in many other cultures too: the Hindu god Kali – a personification of time and change – has taken on a deliberately monstrous appearance in order to terrify. With her flailing arms, wild hair and necklace of heads, she has certainly captured the imagination of generations of artists. Yet one of the aspects of Kali, Durga, is revered in Hinduism as a slayer of demons, and Kali in her softer personifications is widely adored as a mother figure.

Some terrible creatures are the express handiwork of gods, invented for reasons not immediately apparent:

for instance Leviathan and Behemoth, monsters of land and sea mentioned in the Old Testament. A later suggestion that Leviathan could in fact be Satan reveals just how uneasy the relationship between creator and created could be. More obvious was Cerberus' vocation: with his many heads, this enormous hound guarded the entrance to Hades, preventing the curious from entering – and the dead from leaving.

Possibly most monstrous of all are the gods to be found in the Americas, particularly among the Aztecs. Chief among them is Quetzalcoatl, whose name means 'feathered serpent'. Sometimes he is depicted as a snake, though often he wears a red mask with a beak. Tlaloc was another god that could take on horrendous forms, with blue skin, goggle eyes and fangs. The Aztecs, who feared him terribly, would sometimes drown their children to appease him. Xolotl, meanwhile, is most often depicted as having a dog's head, and frequently he is shown with reversed feet.

ymago auaricie fit ꝰe

uertur/

Creature of Chaos

Whereas gods generally represent order, monsters represent chaos. They are violations of the laws of nature since they jumble body parts indiscriminately. 'Chaos' itself is a Greek word, essentially referring to the universe's primordial state – a gaping void or dark abyss where monsters lived before order was imposed upon them. The poet Hesiod describes Chaos as a god, out of whom Erebus (darkness) and Nyx (night) came forth.

The concept seems to be a very old one. An early example of monsters epitomizing chaos is the Babylonian goddess Tiamat. Often depicted as a sea serpent or a dragon – although sometimes featuring other animal parts – she gave birth to the other gods before being killed by the god Marduk. Her body was split into two to form the heaven and the earth: from chaos comes order. And Marduk, by conquering chaos, earns the right to rule over all the other gods. The same notion can also be found in the Bible, where chaos is represented by Leviathan, and where, in the Book of Revelation, the Archangel Michael overpowers Satan, again representing the re-establishment of order.

Even once the order of the gods is settled, chaos can still appear in the form of assaults on the gods' authority. One good example from ancient Mesopotamia is the monstrous bird Anzu, who planned to wrest power away from Enlil, then king of the gods. He stole the tablets of destinies, which tell the future, plunging the gods into chaos. Anzu was eventually slain by the young warrior Ninurta, and order was restored.

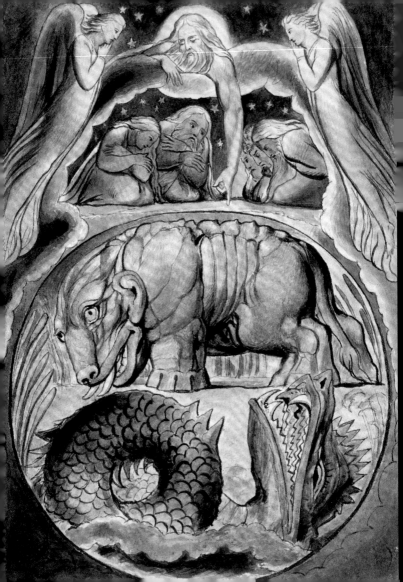

Gods and Monsters

KEY TO ILLUSTRATIONS

2. DEVILS and DEMONS

Demons are perhaps the most enduring monsters of all. From the earliest times people have tended to blame demons whenever something has gone wrong, be it a disastrous harvest or a devastating plague. Ancient Egypt had mischievous demons such as Bes, while Mesopotamia boasted such charming creatures as Pazuzu (who millennia later would become the star of the horror film *The Exorcist*).

While Pazuzu had a clear and terrifying physical form – head of a lion, feet of an eagle, tail of a scorpion – the *djinn* of Arabia and Islam are essentially spirits (according to the Qur'an, they are made from 'smokeless fire'). Demons of this type appear regularly in the Old and New Testaments: Job is tortured by them, while Jesus later casts them out.

Over time, both Judaism and Christianity began to organize these demons into hierarchies, to match the ranks of angels described in the Scriptures. At the top

of the pile sat Satan, the fallen angel who had dared to challenge God. Beneath him were hordes of demons arranged into 'legions' (in Mark 5:8, a demon explains that he is called 'Legion, for we are many'). In 1467 the Spanish bishop Alfonso de Spina calculated that the total number of demons was 133,316,666, but a century later the Dutch demonologist Johann Weyer put the figure at a more conservative 4,439,556, divided into 666 legions, each composed of 6,666 demons. Either way, there were a lot of them.

Since the Bible does not include any physical description of demons, artists were free to invent their own forms. This they did with relish. Often demons appear as smaller versions of Satan; invariably they are as ugly as possible, a mish-mash of different animals given an approximately human shape. Their grotesque appearance tells us that these creatures are up to no good.

By the Middle Ages, demons were depicted everywhere: in manuscripts, in paintings, in the sculpture and stained glass of churches. Grisly scenes of the Last Judgment show sinners bundled off by horrific creatures, while the elect are gathered up by serene angels. Looking at the sheer inventiveness that has gone into depicting these monsters, one cannot help but suspect that the medieval masons rather enjoyed carving them. As it happened, the saints' lives

offered yet more opportunities for depicting devils and demons: one especially popular legend featured St Anthony, who was mercilessly tormented by unpleasant creatures determined to test his faith.

Europe teemed with demons, both seen and unseen, and Asia was similarly infested. Hinduism and Buddhism recognize several categories of demon, ranging from the evil, shape-shifting *rakshasa* to the more ambivalent *asura*. Indian miniatures often show hordes of rather dim-looking demons being knocked about like skittles by stout heroes.

In Japan, the concept of demons can be expanded to cover any number of supernatural creatures. As elsewhere, these *oni* (as they are known) can be either helpful or evil. Although originally conceived as invisible spirits, they gradually took on the appearance of humanoid ogres and are often depicted with horns (not unlike many European demons and devils) and carrying an iron club.

Hellish Creatures

ARTISTS HAVE CONSTANTLY surpassed themselves in their depictions of the Devil's cohorts and minions. In Christian iconography, they appear in scenes showing the Descent into Limbo (which often include the Mouth of Hell) and at the Last Judgment, as well as in episodes from the lives of certain saints (chief among them St Anthony). Any artist commissioned to produce a new Last Judgment would surely have begun with the monsters: whereas angels were properly divine and had a more or less officially recognized form, the Church would be less fussy what the devils and demons looked like, as long as they served to strengthen the resolve and piety of the congregation.

The church of St Mary in Fairford, England, is famous for its stained-glass demons, and early Renaissance art in the Netherlands and Spain contained some astonishingly inventive examples. The master of the monstrous, however, was undoubtedly Hieronymus Bosch. Even today, in the wake of Surrealism and all that modern art has thrown at us, his images are shocking. Their intricate detail draws us closer, into a web of vice and punishment. We see bizarre animals, giant birds, limbs mutating into branches or other objects, bodies hollowed out and inhabited. These demons are no longer straightforward demons, but monstrous hybrids, symbols of a life wasted on sin.

REDEMPTIO

Apoc. C. 9

Vers. 55.

The Many Faces of Satan

AT THE CENTRE OF THE RINGS of demons sits Satan – the Devil, Lucifer, Beelzebub, the Prince of Darkness, the Antichrist. In fact, these different names refer to subtly different characters, who over time have become rolled together to create an all-in-one package of ultimate evil. What seems certain is that this chief opponent of good originally worked for God. However, pride led him to mount a rebellion against his creator, who as punishment consigned him to Hell, along with the angels who had backed him.

Of these various names, the most authentic is Satan, which, alongside 'devil', is used extensively in the Bible. Its origin is obscure, but it may mean 'prosecutor' or 'adversary'. In the New Testament Satan appears to Christ in the wilderness to offer him the riches of the world and to test his goodness ('Get thee behind me, Satan' was Christ's response). From this, the Church developed the idea of Satan as the tempter, trying to ensnare us in our daily lives.

The name Lucifer, often associated with the morning star, means 'light-bringer'; some believed that it was Satan's original name when he was an angel. The name Beelzebub, meanwhile, means 'Lord of the Flies'; some commentators equate Beelzebub with Satan, or else see him as one of Satan's chief assistants. The term 'Antichrist' comes from the biblical Book of Revelation, where he appears as a key figure at the end of times.

Artists had to make Satan's physical appearance match his capacity for evil. Our modern conception of the Devil – tail, bat wings and assorted bits of goat – came about in stages. The wings he presumably kept from his time as an angel, while the elements of goat – sometimes a head, sometimes legs – could derive either from the ancient god Pan or simply from a long line of hybrid monstrosities. The tail, on the other hand, may be a reference to the Beast described in the Book of Revelation.

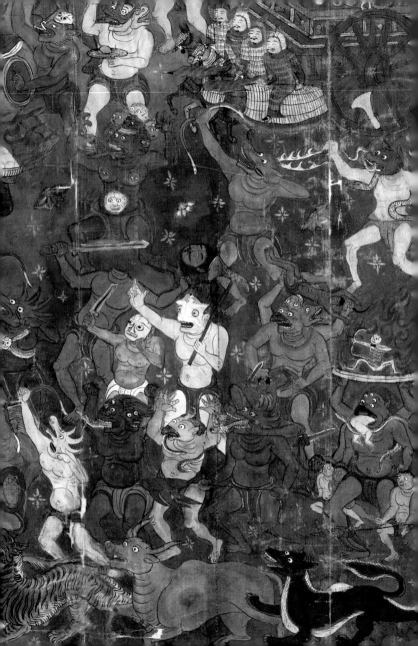

Devils and Demons

KEY TO ILLUSTRATIONS

3. MAGICAL MONSTERS

Monsters and magic have always been closely related. Both deal with the supernatural, both exist outside the day-to-day, and both are widely believed in, even if they are only rarely – if ever – witnessed. Some monsters are the result of magic, whereas others possess magical powers themselves.

Stories of sorcerers communing with demons can be found around the world. Summoning unearthly creatures has long been the domain of witches and wizards: with the aid of grimoires – books of spells and incantations – they would conjure up demons who could advise or aid them. It was believed that other sorcerers could change their shape, assuming animal characteristics, while witches had familiar spirits that could sometimes take diabolical forms.

But some wanted to *create* monsters, not just to summon them, thus stepping on the prerogative of the gods. Alchemists, for example, tried to make 'homunculi' – tiny people grown in flasks. As with most alchemical experiments, success was limited, although that did not stop them trying. The magic books detailing alchemists' dabblings in the occult show a wide range of dragons and other supernatural beasts that take on a new life as symbols of arcane knowledge.

The alchemists were not the only ones to use magic to create life. In Jewish lore, a golem is a creature made by man from inanimate matter and brought to life with an incantation. The most famous example is that supposedly created by a rabbi in late 16th-century Prague to defend against anti-Semitic attacks. To bring the clay creature to life, the rabbi wrote on its forehead the word *emet*, meaning 'truth' or 'reality' in Hebrew. And when he wanted the golem to stop, he rubbed out the first 'e' to leave *met* – the word for 'death'. This theme was continued in Mary Shelley's *Frankenstein*, whose ultimate lesson was that we should not mess with such things: God creates perfect lifeforms; man can create only flawed monsters.

Monsters also have magical properties themselves. Creatures such as unicorns, for example

– whose existence was widely accepted in the Middle
Ages – were a powerful source of magic; their horn
was known to be an antidote to poison. The head of
the snake-haired gorgon Medusa possessed remarkable
properties even after her death at the hands of Perseus:
it could turn people who looked at it to stone. Chinese
dragons (who are considerably more benevolent than
their Western cousins) have long been accredited
with supernatural powers, being able to change their
form and to control the weather.

Others monsters are closely connected to
their magical environments. The figure of Caliban,
in Shakespeare's *The Tempest*, lives on Prospero's
enchanted island. He is the son of a witch and a devil,
and both his peculiar parents and the magical isle seem
to have affected his physical appearance ('What have
we here? A man or a fish?' asks one of the characters).
Artists were drawn to depict this strange, malformed
savage. Shakespeare also calls Caliban a 'mooncalf',

which suggests it was the influence of the lunar cycle that gave him his form – a widely held belief about medical deformities (known then as 'monsters') in Elizabethan times.

Monsters have been evoked in ritual across the globe, most often through the use of masks – a particularly common practice in parts of Africa and the South Pacific. These rites, often shamanistic in nature, take us back to the original prehistoric rituals held in caves underground, designed to create an atmosphere of fear and tension.

Monsters as Protectors

SOME MONSTERS COULD be used on amulets – small objects that keep the wearer or owner safe from harm. For example, the ancient Mesopotamian demon Pazuzu, with his eagle's feet, lion's head and scorpion's tail, was widely feared, but he did have one redeeming feature: he was the enemy of the even less pleasant Huwawa. Since Huwawa was associated with problems in pregnancy, women expecting children wore an amulet in the shape of Pazuzu. Better the devil you know – literally.

Similarly, the head of the gorgon Medusa, cut off by Perseus, possessed a valuable protective quality: those who looked on it turned to stone. The power of the image was used to humanity's advantage, and depictions of Medusa's head were hung in homes and temples to ward off evil spirits. Countless examples of the 'gorgoneion' (as the image is called) have been found throughout the ancient world, including a terrifying terracotta tablet from Sicily. One look at her lolling eyes, protruding tongue and fearsome fangs would make even the most evil of spirits think twice before approaching. Even the goddess Athena wore a depiction of Medusa's head on her shield. Centuries later, various grotesques such as the Sheela-na-Gigs and gargoyles that appear on medieval churches may also have some sort of function in warding off evil.

Another monster that can sometimes offer protection is the *kala*, found in parts of South-East Asia, notably Java. Generally depicted in the form of a fearsome head, it appears above doorways as a guardian spirit. It typically has bulging eyes, rows of sharp fangs and small claws; according to legend, the *kala* devoured the rest of its body on the orders of Shiva, who was appalled at its desire for human flesh.

Magical Monsters
KEY TO ILLUSTRATIONS

4. DRaGons And flYing MONsterS

The dragon has one of the most venerable pedigrees of all monsters. For centuries a heraldic beast in the West – a suitable foe for fearless knights and saints – in the East it has long been associated with emperors. Many writers have pointed out that the two types of dragon – Eastern and Western – for all their similarities belong to very different traditions, but almost certainly both share a common origin in humankind's long-standing fear of reptiles, and of snakes in particular.

Aside from being ancient, dragons are incredibly widespread – so widespread that we might expect to find a skeleton or two. Stories of dragons soon travelled from China to neighbouring Japan, Korea and Malaya, but also as far away as Persia, where, true to form, they were found fighting brave warriors.

HERCULES

LYRA

CYGNUS

CEPHEUS

TARANDUS

CAMELEOPARDALIS

Etamin

Rastaban
vel Alwaid

Cor Kakis

Grumium

ed Asich

Kochab

Cynosura vel Alrucaba
the Polar Star

Errai

Giansar

Sid.ᵗ Hall, sculp.ᵗ

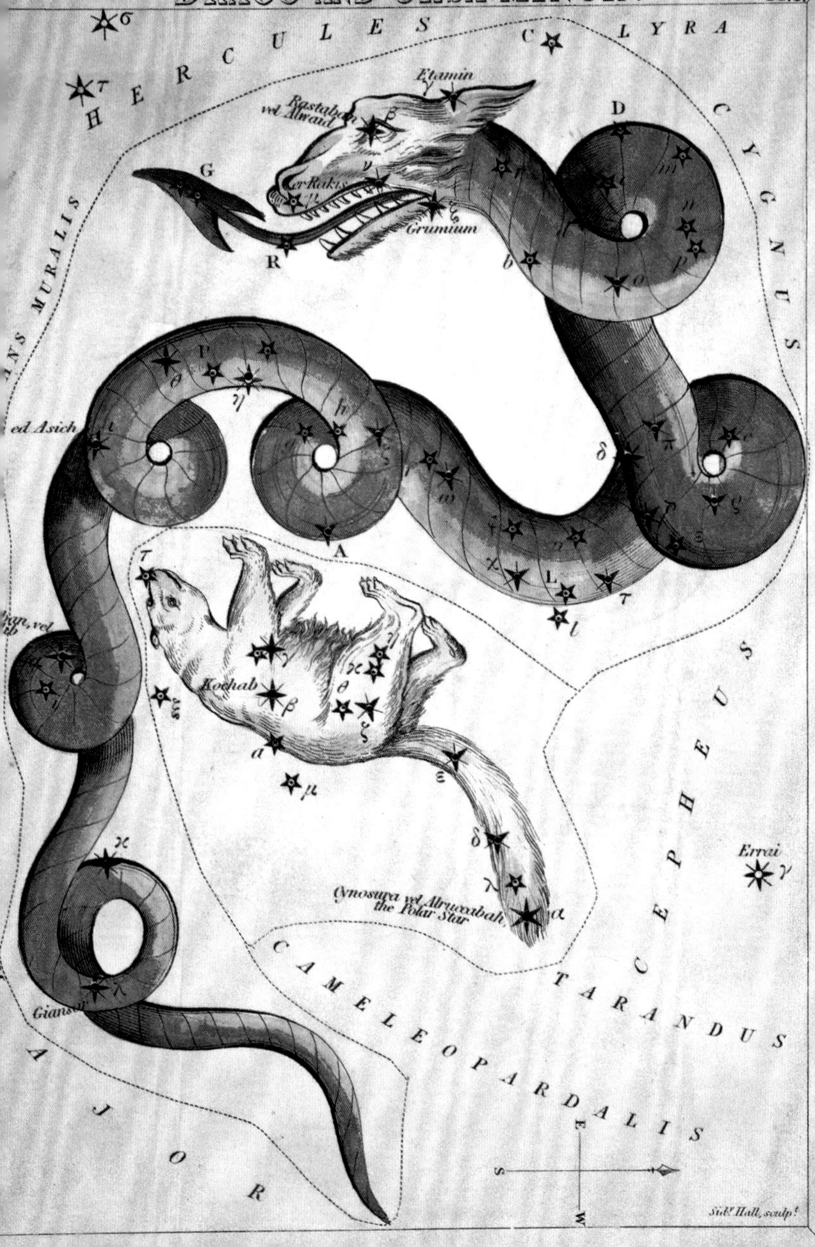

In the West, meanwhile, dragons proliferated throughout Northern and Central Europe, especially in mountainous regions such as Wales and the Alps. Switzerland was long a favoured home for these creatures – the 17th-century writer Athanasius Kircher reports the case of a man who was held hostage by a dragon in the mountains (he eventually escaped by holding onto the beast's tail as it swooped down from its lair). Germany, meanwhile, has for centuries been terrorized by the Lindwurm, a type of dragon that resembles a monstrous snake.

Dragons are far from being the only airborne monsters, however. Perhaps because for most of our history we have been stuck on the ground, winged creatures have always held a special terror for us. Legends of monstrous birds, for example, can be found all over the globe. Perhaps the most famous giant bird is the roc, found in *Arabian Nights*. Large enough to seize and devour elephants, it attacked Sinbad's ship and carried him off to its lair. This legend probably had its origins in another, older Indian legend, of a gigantic bird called Garuda, a lesser Hindu divinity.

Related to these birds is the griffin, which has the body of a lion and the head and wings of an eagle. Often they also boast prominent ears, like those of a horse. And in Russia there exists a famous pair of hybrid bird–humans, called Sirin and Alkonost. Both

sing, but mortals who hear them forget whatever they are doing and follow them – often to their deaths. 'Sirin', of course, recalls the Greek sirens.

In fact, the skies support a whole ecosystem of winged monsters. Appalling furies, screeching harpies and a vast horde of Japanese creatures all circle overhead. Perhaps most curious of all are the winged demons that abound in Northern European art of the 15th and 16th centuries: their wings are so small that they must have to flap as fast as hummingbirds to stay airborne.

Oriental Dragons

THE LEGENDARY FIRST EMPEROR OF CHINA, Huang Di, had a snake as his coat of arms. Fond of conquering other tribes and of asserting his authority, every time somebody fell to him he bolted that tribe's animal emblem onto his own. In time the snake turned into a creature ever more and more monstrous and bizarre – and thus was born the dragon. So goes the popular legend, even if few believe it today. The Oriental dragon is said to have the horns of a deer, the eyes of a demon, the neck of a snake, the claws of a hawk, the ears of a cow, and possibly the belly of a frog and the scales of a carp. And we even know how many scales it has: 117 (81 positive yang, 36 negative yin).

Even if the dragon's origins were 'man-made', it did not take long for people to start believing in them, nor for the dragon to become one of the most potent monsters in countries such as China, Japan and Korea. In Far Eastern cultures, dragons are (generally) benevolent creatures, in spite of their startling appearance, all bulging eyes and open, oversized jaws. Unlike their Western counterparts, they tend not to have wings, but fly instead by some magical force. And unlike in the West, where two-legged dragons are sometimes encountered, Chinese dragons always have four legs. While dragons in Japan and China occasionally breathe fire, generally they are associated with water, and are held responsible for clouds and storms.

SATANAS

Western Dragons

THE EUROPEAN DRAGON is a different beast from its Oriental
counterpart. Dragons first appear in Greek mythology (in the
story of Jason, for example), but our modern conception of them
combines two separate traditions: the *worm* (also called *wyrm*
or *wurm*, a monstrous serpent) and the *draco* (the serpent of the
Garden of the Hesperides or the dragon killed by Cadmus), in
whose honour a constellation was named.

In North and Central Europe we find the Midgard Serpent
of Nordic mythology, battling against Thor and holding the
world together, and in parts of Germany the legend of the
Lindwurm. Unlike normal giant serpents, however, these two
could often breathe fire. In the Anglo-Saxon epic *Beowulf*, the
hero encounters and defeats an unnamed dragon, while in the
German *Nibelungenlied* Siegfried slays a beast that was jealously
guarding a hoard of gold – a common habit among Western
dragons. (The bat-winged *cuélebre* of northern Spain was
particularly possessive.) The Wawel dragon of Cracow, Poland,
is well known for its fondness for devouring young girls, but all
of them pose active threats to humankind, and think nothing of
raiding the nearest town when the cupboards are bare.

The dragon took on its more familiar character – with wings,
scales and distinctive muzzle – in the Middle Ages, as seen
in countless depictions of St George, and by the 15th century
the creature that has come down to us today was more or less
fixed. By and large, dragons in the West are evil yet cunning, but
they can also have magical properties: both Cadmus and Jason
discovered that sowing dragon's teeth grows hardy soldiers.

And after Siegfried had bathed in the dragon's blood, he
became invincible (except, that is, for one part of his shoulder
that had been covered by a leaf).

Dragons and Flying Monsters

KEY TO ILLUSTRATIONS

5.
WATER
MONSTERS

If there is one place on our planet where monsters are likely to exist, it is the vast oceans. Water covers two-thirds of the planet's surface and is home to some of its weirdest and largest creatures. After all, who could conceive of anything as terrifying as the giant squid or the great white shark? Until relatively recently, our knowledge of the seas was very sketchy and superficial; anything could be lurking down there. Sailors, stuck at sea for months at a time, were quick to swap tales of appalling beasts and sea serpents.

References to sea monsters are found from very early on. In Classical mythology, Perseus, fresh from slaying the hideous gorgon Medusa, has to rescue Andromeda from the sea monster Ceto. In Homer's

Odyssey, composed in the late 8th century BC, the long-suffering Odysseus and his crew were obliged to steer a careful course between Scylla and Charybdis; the former ate sailors who came too close, while the latter had a single gaping maw that dragged ships into a vast whirlpool. And sirens and mermaids, although they have occasionally helped humankind, more often have been a hindrance.

The Old Testament book of Job names Leviathan as a giant of the sea: 'Canst thou draw out leviathan with an hook?', it asks, rhetorically. Judging by the description given – 'Out of his mouth go burning lamps, and sparks of fire leap out' – it seems unlikely. Today scholars assume that the inspiration for Leviathan was a whale, but for centuries it was equated with the Devil.

As late as the 16th or even the 17th centuries, we find maps teeming with improbable creatures, many of which look suspiciously like land animals but with flippers and fins. We also come across real animals being mistaken for supernatural creatures – the squid was regarded as a 'sea monk', for instance, and for centuries the narwhal tusks that washed up on the beach were sold for huge sums of money as unicorn's horns. Dried-out skates (known in England as 'Jenny Hanivers') were presented as demonic beings, while the circus impresario P. T. Barnum famously

toured his (highly dubious and very hideous) 'Feejee Mermaid'. For the most part, however, from the 18th century onwards cartographers' oceans were left bare, as humanity reluctantly accepted that sea dragons and sea serpents were a lot less common than previously imagined.

It is not just open sea that is home to monsters. Many inland lakes around the world have their own creatures, the most famous being Loch Ness. While Nessie seems to be fairly benign, Scotland is also home to kelpies, a type of water-dwelling horse whose main pastime seems to be luring unsuspecting passers-by to a watery grave. Japan, another sea-girt nation, has plenty of water-based monsters, although its best known – the tricky, treacherous *kappa* – are found in ponds and rivers.

Kappa

THE KAPPA IS A JAPANESE water spirit of decidedly mixed virtues. On one hand they are courteous to an extreme, always stick to their word, read and speak Japanese, and can be terribly useful around the farm. On the other hand, they love to look up women's kimonos and adore the taste of human flesh (especially children). While, as monsters go, they are among the more civilized, they don't make ideal pets.

Kappa – the name means 'water-child' – can take many forms, although most are about the size of a small child, with webbed hands and feet. Some look a little like frogs; others have duck bills or scaly skin; and some look more like evil tortoises. They come in a variety of colours. One feature that all *kappa* have is a depression in the top of their heads, which is filled with water and surrounded by a curiously tonsured haircut. It is this water that gives them their strength, especially when they leave their natural habitat (a pond or river).

As it happens, this cranial pool is often also the *kappa*'s undoing. Since they are so very polite, and great sticklers for etiquette, they will always bow if bowed to. And when they bow the water spills out, rendering them harmless, immobile or even dead.

Kappa are frequently depicted in Japanese prints of the 18th and 19th centuries, by such artists as Toriyama Sekien or Utagawa Kuniyoshi. Often they are shown wrestling with heroes. Catching a *kappa* can be difficult, though baring your bottom towards it can help provoke an attack.

Incidentally, if you do ever get caught by a *kappa*, it is worth remembering that there is one thing it enjoys even more than the flesh of children: cucumbers.

PARS

PXXXIII 88
MES V 88
PAXXIII 87
MESIIII 87
PXXXI 86
MESIIII 86
PXXX 8c
HVITSARK MESIIII 8+
PXXIX 83
CLIMXVI
MES II 82
PXXVIII 81
PXXVII

FALCO
ALBI

CRIPTODISTICVS

VESTRA
BORDI

MON
CHIVS

VR SI ALBI

ISLANDIA

MARE GLACIALE

SCALHOLDIN

MONHELLA

MOPS SACIS

VALLEN

HEKLA
MON

ARGEN
TEA ET
MEI ECCLE

PISTR. SIVE
PHISET

HORVEGI

AMBRA
SPERMA
CETI

FARE

ZIPHIVS

STR MDXXXVII VISVM

MICHAELIS IN
IETRA SCORDVM
MICHAELIST DE
INSVLIS

TILE

D

BALENA

ORCHA

HEBRIDES
ANIDES
SVS
XL

ORCAD
ESXXXIII

HET LADIA

POMONA

REGVM
ATIVE SEPVLT

MARE
DEVCALIDONICVM

VERMIS 40 PE

HIS CLIPEIS SIGNA PONES VIRTVTIS SORTA
VT PROMTAS GENERIS EXCEAT IPSA TVI

SECVR PARVA

Sirens and Marmaids

Our modern conception of the mermaid is one familiar from Disney: half human, half fish, and fundamentally well intentioned. However, this friendly, romanticized picture glosses over millennia of unease and some pretty unpleasant monsters. Given humankind's ambivalent relationship with the seas, as a source of food and adventure but also of peril, it is not surprising that most mermaids around the globe have similarly combined the roles of helper and adversary.

One of the first mermaid types, complete with a fish's tail, can be recognized in the ancient Syrian goddess Atargatis. Sirens, meanwhile, first appear in a well-known episode from Homer's *Odyssey*, in which those who hear their hypnotic song are drowned. According to Greek legend, they had a taste for human flesh: Homer describes them as surrounded by 'heaps of rotting corpses, skin shrivelling on their bones'. Despite the fact that the siren soon became conflated with the mermaid (in many romance languages, the word for 'mermaid' is *sirena, sirène, syrena* or similar), sirens do not actually live in the sea, and instead are winged creatures with birds' talons instead of fishtails. The singing mermaid motif caught on, however, and is now a motif in most tales involving sirens, including the *Arabian Nights.*

There have been many local variations over the years. The Finnish water spirit known as Näkki – beautiful from the front, but ugly from behind – pulls children to their depths, while Slavic mythology has the Vodyanoy: an old man with black scales, webbed paws and burning red eyes, who delights in flooding the land. Other traditions have mermen, often with hair of seaweed, though they seem to show no interest in the affairs of humankind.

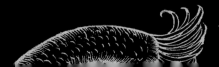

Water Monsters
KEY TO ILLUSTRATIONS

6.
tRaNsFoRMaTiONs
aNd HyBRIDS

One of the more unnerving properties of monsters is their ability to change their form. Shape-shifting can be found in many mythologies around the world: the Nordic god Odin could turn himself into an eagle, and Loki into a salmon, while Zeus routinely assumed other forms to trick gods and mortals.

The Roman poet Ovid was the most enthusiastic cataloguer of transformations – indeed, his best-known work is called *Metamorphoses*. Many of the monsters that we encounter in Ovid sound as though they have been halted halfway through changing: one famous example is the Minotaur, the result of an affair between Minos' wife Pasiphaë and an enchanted bull. Later on, magical transformations become a staple of fairy tales: the spell is broken and the beast returns to human form. Alternatively, humans are turned into monsters

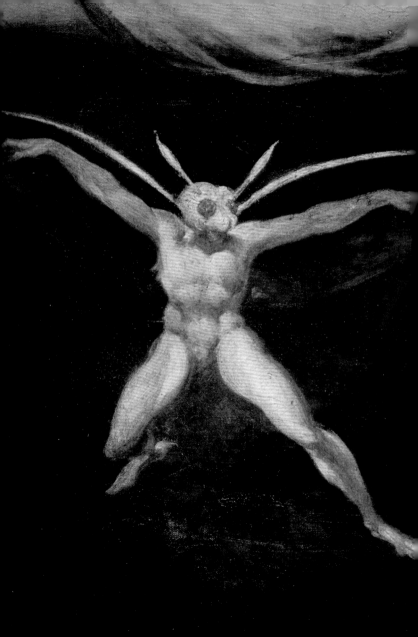

as a punishment – as happens with Svipdagr, who is changed into a dragon by Odin.

In China and Japan it was widely believed that foxes could change themselves into men, normally to trick real humans. The Japanese *bakeneko* (ghost cat) can either walk on its hind legs or turn itself into human form; it terrorizes houses with fireballs and sometimes devours the owner, taking its place. In the Philippines, the most feared monster by far is the *aswang*, an evil vampire-type creature that can appear as a large black dog or a bear. It has a taste for blood, but can be beaten off with a stingray's tail or warded off with garlic. Often these transformations are not voluntary: take werewolves, for example, which are locked into an inescapable cycle linked to the moon.

Most monsters are hybrids, but many of the most chilling combine a human body with the head of an animal – the Minotaur is a good example, as are many of the Egyptian gods (the jackal-headed Anubis even today appears in horror films). The earliest such representations can be found in prehistoric caves, but most of the hybrid monsters we know today have their origins in the ancient Near East.

Legends of cynocephaly – human beings with a dog's head – are found around the world, and for centuries it was believed that a whole race of dog-headed people lived in India. Even more bizarre are the depictions of St Christopher with the head of a dog found in the Orthodox Church – possibly to reflect his out-of-the-way origins, and possibly because of inventive and badly translated narratives of his life.

These images are unsettling precisely because we know that inside the animal head is the brain of a human. We find the combination of animal savagery with the cunning and malice of a human mind particularly terrifying. In addition, several commentators have seen monsters and hybrids as reflecting a human preoccupation with retaining mastery over the animal kingdom.

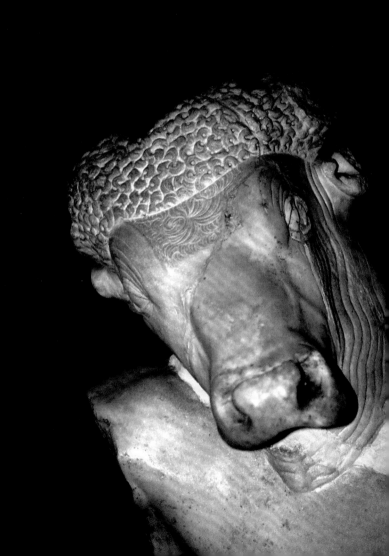

Demon Foxes

FOR THE JAPANESE, foxes were to be treated with
great suspicion. For although they generally posed a
threat only to chickens, there was a chance that any
fox one encountered could turn out to belong to a breed of
supernaturals. These foxes, known as *kitsune*, over the years
gained the ability to walk upright and eventually to transform
themselves into human form, often choosing to appear as
beautiful women. For this reason they were classified as a
type of transforming *yokai* (supernatural spirit). (Other stories
tell how foxes, with advancing years, gained more tails – up
to a maximum of nine.) Once in human form – which the foxes
achieved by holding a skull over their heads – they would
generally set about causing trouble.

Other mischievous foxes could transform themselves into
more terrifying creatures. The illustrations opposite relate
to the story of Ooishi Hyoroku. This young warrior declared to
his friends that he would prove his mettle by going on a quest.
However, some foxes overheard him, and decided to lie in wait
to scare him. So as he went on his journey, from time to time the
foxes, having assumed monstrous form, would jump out, and
Hyoroku would run off, terrified.

What could be done about the foxes? The answer
was to erect shrines to the fox god, Inari. Even today,
about one third of all Shinto shrines in Japan are
dedicated to Inari, and people leave offerings
of food to appease the fox spirits.

Werewolves

MOST MONSTERS are born rather than made monstrous, but not so the werewolf. Instead, a human becomes a werewolf through contact with another werewolf, by putting on a particular item (often a belt of wolfskin, or even the creature's pelt) or occasionally through some potion or ointment (the latter being particularly popular during the Middle Ages).

One of the earliest stories of wolfish transformation is told by Ovid, who relates how the cruel King Lycaon was punished by Jupiter for serving up his children as dinner. (His name is related to the Greek *lykos*, which means 'wolf' and which gives us the term 'lycanthrope'.) However, the defining feature of the werewolf is that it oscillates between being human and animal; the change is not permanent. The Classical writer Herodotus writes of a Scythian tribe who turned into wolves every few years, though he seems to have had his doubts.

Werewolf stories abound throughout Russia and Northern and Central Europe (the Harz Mountains in Germany seem to have been a breeding ground for the creatures). These tales often contain grisly details, which have attracted artists such as Lucas Cranach the Elder. The poem *Bisclavret*, written by Marie de France in the 12th century, tells the story of a man who turns into a wolf every week, and changes back to human form by donning his normal clothes (when his wife steals his clothes he is trapped in the wolf's body). In Mesoamerica similar myths of transformation were based around were-jaguars, while in Haiti they survive as *jé-rouges* ('red eyes'), who behave like vampires in trying to spread their condition. The legend of the werewolf was kept alive by episodes such as the attacks in Gévaudan in 1760s France, in which a wolf-like beast terrorized the local inhabitants.

Transformations and Hybrids

KEY TO ILLUSTRATIONS

7. GHOSTS AND GHOULS

Since monsters contravene the laws of nature and fail to fit into our understanding of the animal kingdom, we have constantly speculated about their physical make-up. Many have arrived at the conclusion that they are a form of spirit or ghost, neither of this world nor of the next. While ghosts in themselves are not necessarily monstrous, they often take on monstrous forms.

In Norse mythology dead Vikings could be accompanied by a spirit called a *draugr*. These creatures hung around graves, especially ones packed with tempting treasure. They had extraordinary strength and could change their size at will; they would hunt and devour the living, though generally they could not stray too far from their grave. They are either blue–black or ghostly white in colour.

A similar spirit crops up in Arabian folklore, where it is called a *ghul*, or 'ghoul'. These demons are

supposedly the children of Iblis (the Islamic Devil); they can shape-shift, sometimes taking the forms of hyenas, and they feast on the flesh of the living (having a particular taste for lost children). Ghouls make their literary debut in the *Arabian Nights*, but the concept spread, and in 1848 Edgar Allen Poe included them in his poem 'The Bells': 'They are neither man nor woman / They are neither brute nor human / They are Ghouls.'

In time, the world 'ghoul' was replaced by the word 'zombie', most often connected to the practice of voodoo in Haiti, in which the dead are brought back to life and then controlled by a *bokor* or sorcerer. The zombies we know today are related to the ancient concept of the 'undead' – corpses that have been reanimated or taken over by vengeful spirits. The modern tale of Frankenstein's monster, first published by Mary Shelley in 1818, is an obvious relation.

Perhaps the most extensive collection of monstrous spirits and ghostly demons can be found in East Asia. There, ancestor worship has meant that a whole tradition of 'hungry ghosts' has emerged – in East Asia they are called *pretas*, and in Japan *gaki*. Not having sufficient food in their afterlife, they come back

to terrify the living and to feed off their fear – which they sometimes achieve by changing their forms.

Not all ghostly creatures are frightening, however, and Japan also has an entire caste of far less fearsome, and often humorous, spirits called *obake*. Literally meaning 'transforming thing', the word is used to describe creatures that inhabit day-to-day objects such as umbrellas or lamps. There is also another class of ghosts called *yurei*: these are less well intentioned, returning to the land of the living to seek vengeance. They are punctual, and most often appear between two and three o'clock in the morning. A further class of Japanese apparition are the *yokai*: these are more conventionally monstrous, and include the well-known *kappa*, the peculiar *rokurokubi* (who look like humans but have rubbery extendable necks) and the *tengu* (a type of mountain goblin).

The Stuff of Nightmares

NIGHT HAS ALWAYS brought with it terror and uncertainty – more so before the era of electricity. Nyx, the primordial goddess of the night, was born of Chaos, and her children included Thanatos (death), Nemesis (retribution), Hypnos (sleep) and Charon (who ferries the dead to Hades). Dreams have long been interpreted as a portal to a greater reality, and in the ancient world they were scrutinized for portents and warnings (the original meaning of the English 'monster'). Thus the connection between dreams, night and monsters has always been strong.

For this reason, monsters are often depicted in a dreamlike context. One image from the Renaissance, *The Dream* (1544) by Battista Dossi, features a sleeping woman surrounded by peculiar and disturbing creatures that seem to fuse human and shellfish body parts. The attendant owl recalls the strix – a Classical bird of ill omen that supped on human blood. But perhaps the greatest depiction of the terrors of the night is that by Henry Fuseli called *The Night Mare* (1781). In this wonderfully Gothic painting, a strange creature sits on the chest of a young woman who looks more fainted from terror than asleep. The goblin-like apparition stares straight at the viewer, yet it is the ghostly horse that steals the scene, with its blind, shining eyes. Sigmund Freud had a print of this very painting on the wall of his study, and even wrote a paper on it.

Perhaps the most astute comment on the dangers of falling prey to fear, however, comes from the Spanish artist Francisco Goya. In his print 'The Sleep of Reason Breeds Monsters', a man, fast asleep, has let go of his rationality and is already in the clutches of some rather creepy-looking creatures.

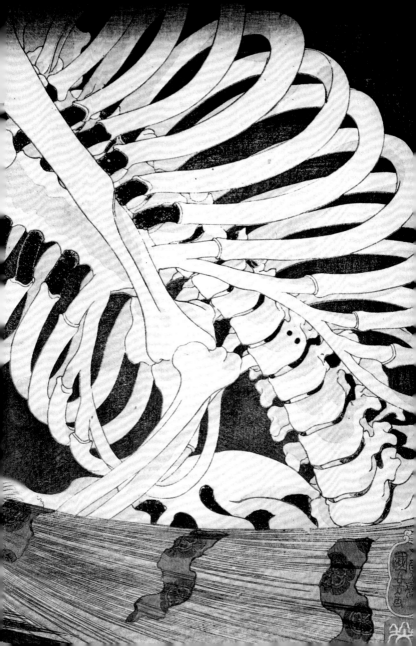

El sueño de la razón produce monstruos.

Ghosts and Ghouls

KEY TO ILLUSTRATIONS

8.
MONSTERS
OF FOLKLORE

The legends of folklore are those born of long nights gathered around fires. Reflecting a more superstitious time – or at least a time when the world held more wonder – these stories invariably feature both magic and monsters. The monsters in folklore are the beasts of deserted clearings in forests, of lonely desolate places beyond the outskirts of town, or they lie in wait for unwary travellers. The folklore tradition is an oral one, meaning that stories can mutate, and monsters can gain extra heads, longer tails and even sharper teeth just in a retelling.

Since these monsters live in the imagination, some of them are fairly wild. One folk monster from the Philippines, the *manananggal*, can detach its legs and fly off on night-time prowls. It can be killed by locating the legs and sprinkling ashes or garlic on them.

Legends can develop quickly, and every now and again a peculiar event will spark a new tale.

One famous example is the Beast of Gévaudan, which was the subject of local hysteria and a lengthy hunt between 1764 and 1767. Some eighty deaths, attributed to an animal that resembled a wolf but was significantly larger, led the king himself to send in a team of soldiers. They wiped out most of the area's wolves, and the attacks stopped.

The 18th and 19th centuries in North America saw a crowd of new monsters, discovered by loggers as they penetrated the thick forests on their way to the west coast. Known as the 'fearsome critters', they included peculiar and terrifying beasts such as the axehandle hound (a dog that ate axe handles – one wonders what they lived on before the woodcutters arrived). Pennsylvania had the hideously ugly squonk, which would burst into tears if caught, while Wisconsin was home to the savage, dinosaur-like hodag (sadly revealed to be a hoax). All appeared in William T. Cox's *Fearsome Creatures of the Lumberwoods,* published in 1910. In very recent years new myths have emerged, such as the goat-devouring *chupacabra* in Mexico, and the mothman, allegedly seen in West Virginia in 1966–67.

Monsters also play an important role in local festivities, including those of a religious nature. In Tarascon, southern France, annual processions commemorate the triumph of St Martha over the

159

six-legged Tarasque (a sort of dragon with elements of tortoise). The townspeople parade a startling effigy of the creature, most often with a man wedged in its mouth, through the streets. In Catalonia and Valencia, models of devils and dragons are often paraded at important feasts, while in some Alpine regions the horned figure of Krampus acts as a sort of anti-St Nicholas, punishing naughty children where Santa Claus rewards them. The Krampus masks and costumes are terrifying even by today's standards. In these acts monsters are at once celebrated and lampooned.

The Night Parade
of 100 Demons

ACCORDING TO JAPANESE folk belief, one night every summer
monsters parade through the streets. Known in Japanese as
Hyakki Yako, this procession gave artists free rein to depict what
they fancied – dancing cats, animated furniture, all manner of
ghost, demon and devil, distorted faces and masks – and plenty
of things that defy description.

The Night Parade became popular in the 18th century with
the publication of a book written and illustrated by Toriyama
Sekien. Sekien, a scholar as well as an accomplished artist,
decided to catalogue all known types of ghost and monster –
a project that in Japan could run to many volumes. The first
volume was published in 1781 under the title *The Night Parade
of 100 Demons*. The creatures depicted by Sekien and his
contemporaries are generally the supernatural monster-spirits
known as *yokai*. These include the *kappa*, the rubbery *rokorukubi*
and the winged *tengu*: not exactly harmless, but capable of
fun. However, Sekien also included *oni* – ogre-type creatures
normally wielding clubs – who have less of a sense of humour,
and in some Buddhist traditions are responsible for punishing
wrongdoers in hell.

Related to the belief in demons was the popular parlour game
known as 'the gathering of one hundred supernatural tales'.
Played by samurai as a test of courage, it began with the lighting
of one hundred candles. The guests took turns to tell a ghost
story, and after each story one candle was extinguished.
Finally, when the last candle had flickered out, the monsters
would arrive ...

Monsters of Folklore

KEY TO ILLUSTRATIONS

9. How to fight monsters

'Whoever fights monsters should take care not to become one,' warned the German philosopher Friedrich Nietzsche. In our determination to destroy our fears, he is saying, we run the risk of becoming even worse than them. Yet monsters are there to be fought, struggled against and resisted – and have been since the beginning of civilization.

The natural enemy of the monster is the hero. The 'hero myth', which can be found in just about every culture and in every period, from Greece to Japan, usually involves some sort of threat – normally in the form of a monstrous or otherwise terrible creature – that the locals or gods despair of defeating. Every possible approach has been tried,

and sometimes the very foundations of society seem threatened. Then along comes the hero who, through either cunning or (more often) brute strength and valour, overcomes the beast and restores order.

One of the earliest of such myths occurs in the *Enûma Elish*, the creation text of ancient Mesopotamia. It relates how the monster-goddess Tiamat, determined to avenge a killing, gives birth to sea serpents, dragons, merpeople, storm demons and scorpion men. The deities hold an emergency meeting and panic. Then one of the minor deities, Enlil (or, in later versions, Marduk), promises to kill the monsters in return for being recognized as the king of the gods. So upon locating Tiamat, 'with his merciless club he smashed her skull'.

The ancient Greeks had their own heroic monster-slayer, Hercules, who, in addition to performing his Twelve Labours, is also sometimes credited as helping Theseus overcome the Minotaur. In fact, Hercules was following in the footsteps of his grandfather Perseus, who had decapitated Medusa and saved Andromeda from a sea monster on the way home. Hercules' sometime companion Jason (who was educated by a monster, the centaur Chiron) overcame the sleepless dragon that guarded the Golden Fleece with the help of a magic potion; in some versions he was devoured and then regurgitated by the beast.

When Jason and his crew encountered the sirens
(the same who had caused Odysseus so much grief),
Orpheus drowned out their singing with his lyre.

As these examples show, violence need not be
the only way to beat monsters. Another Classical
example is that of Oedipus and the Sphinx (another
of Echidna's horrible offspring). One could defeat this
creature of death and destruction only by correctly
answering her riddle. Oedipus chanced his luck and
won, whereupon the monster killed herself. Relying
on more orthodox tricks, the Nordic god Thor
captured the Midgard Serpent (briefly) while on
a fishing trip, using a bull's head as bait.

Other monsters can be caught or killed with
very specific, sometimes magical, tools. Vampires
are traditionally warded off by garlic and killed with
a stake through the heart. Werewolves, on other hand,
are susceptible to silver bullets. The *cuélebre* dragon
of Asturias has swordproof scales but can be killed by
being fed a red-hot stone or bread stuffed full of pins.

Other monsters can be resisted through faith
alone. The Bible may not be very specific about
monsters, but the lives of the saints are full of grisly
beasts. In some cases they are clearly agents or
emblems of the Devil, and the task of the saint is to
rid humanity of the beast. St Martha was initially
devoured by the Tarasque, but escaped (echoing the

太田但馬政が
　廣政の良筆に
政の良筆に
十
この
命ぶ依て
の時早太
江戸宵合といふ
二刀と勇名と。

rebirth of Christ) and led it into the town. Just as the Devil could be repelled by saying 'Vade retro satana' – 'Go back, Satan' – and vampires driven back by crucifixes, so too could faith provide protection against the evils of the world.

Hercules

WHEN IT COMES to killing monsters, few had the breadth of experience of Hercules. The son of Zeus by a mortal woman, he was for the ancient Greeks the very essence of manhood, fantastically strong, courageous and ingenious. Zeus's wife, Hera, furious at her husband's affair, sent a snake to kill the infant Hercules; but the child, then just a few months old, throttled the snake, thus beginning a long and highly successful career of slaughter.

Hercules is best known for his Twelve Labours – a series of seemingly impossible tasks, several of which involved monsters. His first victim was the Nemean Lion, whose impenetrable pelt he thereafter wore as armour. Next came the appalling Lernaean Hydra, which lived in a swamp and possessed nine heads and poisonous breath. Having covered his mouth to approach the beast, Hercules proceeded to lop off its heads. But every time a head fell, two grew back in its place, so Hercules called on his nephew to cauterize the neck stumps after every swing of his blade. With the monster safely dead, Hercules dipped his arrows in its venomous blood (bound to come in useful later).

Hercules' next major monster was the fearsome giant Geryon, who had three heads, six arms, and either two or six legs But the brute was quickly despatched by an arrow tipped with Hydra blood.

Our hero's final task was perhaps the most taxing: to capture (alive) the hellhound Cerberus, who boasted three snarling heads (or fifty, according to Hesiod) and a mane of live serpents. Discarding the poison-tipped arrows, Hercules simply slung the beast over his back and carried him off.

St George

ST GEORGE IS BY SOME WAY the best-known adversary of dragons. The real George was almost certainly born in Palestine in the 3rd century AD, and was martyred by the Emperor Diocletian in around 302–3. Although the saint was already known in the West, the story became popular when the first Crusaders returned from the Holy Land in the 12th century. Every so often he appears alongside St Demetrius, another warrior saint.

The best account of the saint's fight with the dragon comes from the 13th-century *Golden Legend*, a collection of saints' stories assembled by the Italian monk Jacobus de Voragine. Here, the action takes place in Libya – perhaps considered sufficiently distant and exotic to have such monsters. The dragon had been terrorizing a kingdom for some time, and its appetite had progressed from sheep to children, who were chosen by lottery. One day, as the king's daughter was about to be devoured, St George passed and vowed to destroy the creature. Wounding it with his lance, he then fastened the princess's girdle around the beast's neck. Thus pacified, it was led back to the city by the saint, who persuaded the king to convert to Christianity – and then heroically lopped the dragon's head off.

This is, of course, another battle between order and chaos. George's struggle echoes that of St Michael against the Beast of the Apocalypse (called a 'dragon' in some translations) as told in the Book of Revelation. In the legend of St George, the dragon is probably a metaphor for the Roman Empire, which very soon would convert to Christianity – George's real achievement. He was widely seen in the medieval Church as a champion of chivalry, and is today the patron saint of England, Georgia, Milan, Catalonia, Beirut and Malta, among many other places.

How to Fight Monsters

KEY TO ILLUSTRATIONS

10. OfF thE Edge Of thE mAp

The margins of human knowledge have always been fertile territory for monsters. In his *Natural History*, written in the 1st century AD, the great Roman historian Pliny enthusiastically described the monstrous races that lurked on the fringes of (Roman) civilization. The medieval world saw no reason to doubt his word, even adding their own creations. The strange gods and curious rituals of cultures just off the map were a cause for wonder and fear. And this was as true of Romans looking at India as it was of Japanese contemplating America.

As a result, for centuries science existed alongside superstition. The 16th-century Swiss naturalist Conrad Gessner, for example, is widely credited with producing the first ever proper study of zoology (the *Historiae animalium*), but alongside his descriptions of mundane animals we find apocalyptical beasts

So erscheinet der Belzebub.
Seine Nahmen: Mandragora mit Maußen Jahr

agorS.
rufar
isoso

Turitél.
Nelion
Eloson.

and hydras. A little later, the Italian naturalist Ulisse Aldrovandi was instrumental in founding the modern field of botany, but also found time to write books on monsters (illustrated with suitably far-fetched prints). His near contemporary Ambroise Paré, a leading surgeon of his day, reported on monstrous or prodigious births, attributing deformities to supernatural influence. In his 1573 book *On Monsters and Marvels,* Paré defined monsters as 'things that appear outside the course of Nature'.

These beliefs are not surprising given the period in which the authors lived, at a time when the existence of witchcraft and magic was taken for granted. In fact, the word 'monster' comes from the Latin *monstrum,* meaning 'omen', and for millennia the sort of deformities that interested Paré – conjoined twins, for instance – were thought to be portents or warnings from God. One famous example was a boy born in the late 16th century who had the faces of dogs and cats on his elbows, shoulders and knees, curious feathers growing out of his head, and webbed feet. Although he lived just a few hours, it was thought he foretold the Second Coming of Christ.

Even in the 17th century many scientists were capable of believing in supernatural creatures alongside alchemy. The great Swiss polymath Athanasius Kircher gave credence to reports of dragons

in the Swiss Alps, for instance (even if he was more doubtful about giants in the south of Italy). But Kircher increasingly seemed a relic of a bygone age, and by the 18th century a new scepticism was taking root.

Now that we have mapped and charted most of the world's surface, it seems safe to say that not much remains to be discovered (not on the scale of dragons, at any rate). The study of cryptids – creatures that might or might not exist – has taken off in recent years, but anything that we do find, be it a Bigfoot or a Yeti, is likely to share our evolutionary origins.

Perhaps it is for this reason that the popular imagination has turned to the 'final frontier': outer space. From the earliest science fiction of Jules Verne and H. G. Wells – and ever more rapidly during the 20th century – we have in a sense been transported back to the concept of 'monstrous races': the idea that just beyond our reach lies something truly spectacular.

Monstrous Races

Our earliest account of the 'monstrous races' comes from Pliny's *Natural History*, written in *c.* 77 AD, which attempted to account for the earth's geography, peoples and cultures. It seems Pliny was rather too trusting of his sources, however.

Pliny situates most of his monstrosities in 'India' or 'Ethiopia'. Illyrians are said to possess the evil eye, while satyrs roam 'in the western mountains of India' (the latter, conveniently, are so swift of foot that they can 'never be taken'). The hairy Choromandae make a 'horrible gnashing noise', while others in the same region, Pliny assures us, 'engender with beasts', creating 'monstrous mongrels, half beasts and half men'. It was the mingled blood of a warring elephant and dragon that gave us the mineral cinnabar.

Pliny's work culminates in a race of creatures who feed exclusively on the milk of dog-headed humans called Cynocephalae. He concludes that such creations are Nature's 'pastime', a way of playing with humankind for her own amusement and to 'set us a wondering at such strange miracles'.

Monstrous races became a very popular theme in the Middle Ages. They are depicted in the tympanum of Vézelay Cathedral in France, as well as in dozens of illuminated manuscripts – an expression of God's boundless creativity. But perhaps most comical of all are the Sciapods: these creatures, though remarkably speedy, are most often shown on their backs, using their one giant foot to protect themselves from the fierce sun.

Nelle ultime parte de fricana al fine della terrà sono tal forma se huomini tutti
humani excetò hano el collo de grua el capo bestiale li occhi el naso humano el becco elle
barbole come galli uesteno di pelle e lauorao la terra e fano grà guerra cò li ucelli grifoni per modo che ne moreno grà numero de luno eddaltro le loro donne sono a sua simiglianza
ma nò hano barbole e hano el becco largo e nò beue uino. quelli che moreno nela bataglia sono
tenuti si come sancti. et le loro donne nò se lasano mai piu ueder da huomini.

In alchune ualle della tartaria sono stati trouati tal móstri como qui se uede, hano el collo lógo
sopra el busto, e in cima una testa in forma de grifoni, e nel petto doi occhi, naso e bocca, có doe ale
alli fiachi de diuersi colori, et háno le brazze e gábe humane, et habitano in lochi doue siano aque, e se
uiueno di pesci, uolano graui come le oche e le sue pene dele ale, se adoperano alle frizze de grá signori
maxime el grá cane e delli gentilhuomeni, sono animali ferocissimi, delli huomeni butano ueneno p̄ bocha
quando se uoleno pigliare.

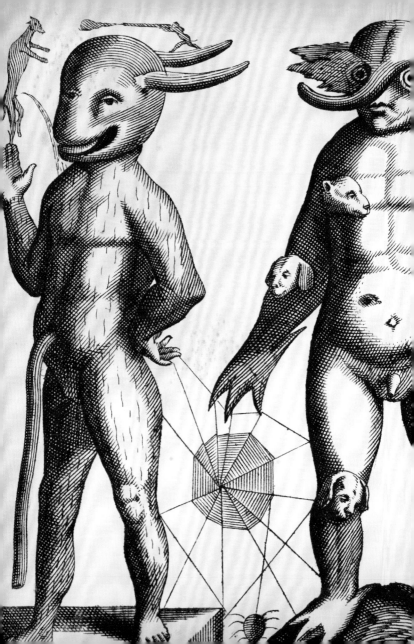

Off the Edge of the Map

KEY TO ILLUSTRATIONS

furthER ReAdiNg

Monsters have fascinated people in many fields, from biologists to philosophers, and from art historians to anthropologists. The following list offers a cross-selection of approaches, from the light-hearted to the deadly serious.

Stephen Asma, *On Monsters: An Unnatural History of our Worst Fears* (New York: Oxford University Press, 2010)

Stéphane Audeguy, *Les Monstres: Si loin et si proches* (Paris: Gallimard, 2007)

R. Barber and A. Riches, *A Dictionary of Fabulous Beasts* (New York: Walker, 1972)

Timothy K. Beal, *Religion and its Monsters* (New York: Routledge, 2002)

Timothy Clark, *Demon of Painting: The Art of Kawanabe Kyosai* (London: British Museum Press, 1991)

Jeffrey J. Cohen, *Monster Theory: Reading Culture* (Minneapolis: University of Minnesota Press, 1996)

Jacob Covey, *Beasts!* (Seattle: Fantagraphics, 2006)

—— *Beasts! Book Two* (Seattle: Fantagraphics, 2008)

Ariane Delacampagne and Christian Delacampagne, *Here Be Dragons: A Fantastic Bestiary* (Princeton, N. J.: Princeton University Press, 2003)

Dorothy Dinnerstein, *The Mermaid and the Minotaur: Sexual Arrangements and Human Malaise* (New York: Other Press, 1999)

Umberto Eco and Alastair McEwen, *On Ugliness* (London: Harvill Secker, 2007)

Richard Ellis, *Monsters of the Sea* (New York: Knopf, 1994)

Michael Dylan Foster, *Pandemonium and Parade: Japanese Monsters and the Culture of Yokai* (Berkeley, Calif.: University of California Press, 2008)

John Block Friedman, *The Monstrous Races in Medieval Art and Thought* (Cambridge, Mass.: Harvard University Press, 1981)

David D. Gilmore, *Monsters: Evil Beings, Mythical Beasts, and All Manner of Imaginary Terrors* (Philadelphia: University of Pennsylvania, 2002)

Elaine L. Graham, *Representations of the Post/Human: Monsters, Aliens and Others in Popular Culture* (Manchester: Manchester University Press, 2002)

Massimo Izzi, *Diccionario ilustrado de los monstruos* (Palma de Mallorca/ Barcelona: José J. de Olañeta, 2000)

Ernest Martin, *Histoire des monstres depuis l'antiquité jusqu'à nos jours* (Paris: C. Reinwald et Cie, 1880)

Monstruos y seres imaginarios (exhibition catalogue, Madrid: Biblioteca Nacional, 2000)

C. Rose, *Giants, Monsters & Dragons: An Encyclopedia of Folklore, Legend & Myth* (New York: W. W. Norton & Company, 2002)

C. J. S. Thompson, *The Mystery and Lore of Monsters* (New York: University Books, 1968)

Mary Wakeman, *God's Battle with the Monster: A Study in Biblical Imagery* (Leiden: Brill, 1973)

Hiroko Yoda, Matt Alt and Tatsuya Morino, *Yokai Attack!: The Japanese Monster Survival Guide* (Tokyo: Kodansha International, 2008)

WEBSITES
There are several websites and blogs dedicated to monsters. The best, by some way (at least for pictures), is monsterbrains.blogspot.com. Other websites worth looking at include:
www.strangescience.net (considers monsters in the history of science)
pinktentacle.com (various aspects of Japanese culture, including much on monsters)
www.golemjournal.org (the online journal *GOLEM: Journal of Religion and Monsters*)

PiCtuRE CRediTs

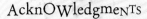

AcknOWledgmeNTs

My biggest thanks go to Rosa and Alex for enduring
hours and hours of monstrous musings, and to Joan
Niella i Casas for his unerring eye for the eerie. I'm
grateful to the staff of various libraries and picture
libraries for their invaluable help in my quest for the
bizarre and little seen. And I'm particularly grateful to
all those individuals who were kind enough to let me
use their own creative efforts. Finally, I'd like to thank
everyone at Thames & Hudson for their support,
patience and unflagging enthusiasm.

First published in the United Kingdom in 2010 by
Thames & Hudson Ltd, 181A High Holborn, London WC1V 7QX

This compact edition 2016
Reprinted 2024

Monsters © 2010 and 2016 Christopher Dell

Cover illustration by David Bezzina

British Library Cataloguing-in-Publication Data
A catalogue record for this book is available from the British Library

ISBN 978-0-500-29255-6

Printed and bound in China by C&C Offset Printing Co. Ltd

FSC MIX Paper FSC® C008047